SOME INFLUENCES IN MODERN
PHILOSOPHIC THOUGHT

Some Influences in Modern Philosophic Thought

By
ARTHUR TWINING HADLEY
President of Yale University

KENNIKAT PRESS, INC./PORT WASHINGTON, N. Y.

SOME INFLUENCES IN MODERN PHILOSOPHIC THOUGHT

Copyright 1913 by Yale University Press
Reissued in 1968 by Kennikat Press

Library of Congress Catalog Card No: 67-27604

Manufactured in the United States of America

Analyzed in the ESSAY & GENERAL LITERATURE INDEX

PREFACE

By the will of the late John Calvin McNair a course of lectures was established at the University of North Carolina whose object should be to show the mutual bearing of science and theology upon each other. It was my privilege to serve as McNair Lecturer in the year 1912.

I have published the lectures substantially as they were delivered; but I have divided what was originally the first lecture into two separate chapters. I have taken the liberty of adding, as an Appendix, a brief discussion of the meaning of the term Philosophy, which has not been hitherto published, and an estimate of the influence of Darwin upon historical and political thought, reprinted from the Psychological Review for May, 1909.

No one can expect to find an exhaustive treatment of so large a topic in so small a space; but I venture to hope that some may be helped in their reading and in their thinking by the suggestions which the book contains.

I am glad to take this opportunity to express my great indebtedness to the faculty and students of the University of North Carolina for the courtesy which I enjoyed during my stay at Chapel Hill.

A. T. H.

Yale University,
December, 1912.

CONTENTS

I

GENERAL PURPOSE OF THE COURSE

A SEARCHING test of what educa-
tion has done for a man is given by
the question: "Has he gained a sense of
the real and permanent values of the different parts of life, as distinct from their
apparent magnitude at the moment?"

This sense is not common, nor easily
acquired. Most men judge the size of
things by their nearness or remoteness.
A single maple tree in the foreground
blots out a hundred miles of distant land-
scape from their minds as well as their
eyes. The man who is occupied with the
pursuit of money or political office or
scientific research tends to think everything
small which does not visibly contribute to
money-getting, or political influence, or

scientific discovery. There is much in the current teaching of the day which tends to increase this danger. We are prone to disparage philosophic methods of study as compared with practical ones; to urge the student to develop his special interests and capacities rather than to widen his intellectual horizon; to count the man as best educated who can best do his own small fraction of the world's work.

With this view I have little sympathy. He who is content to be a specialist and nothing more, however long and well he may have been trained, cannot properly be said to have been educated. This term is by rights reserved for him who has acquired a broad outlook on life as a whole; who has worked out ideas of his own as to the relation between our own selves, the visible universe about us, and the invisible principle that rules it. Ideas of his own, I say. A man cannot take his philosophy at second hand, as a set of ready-made principles based on the study and experience of others. If he tries to do this he gets a creed, not a philosophy. "What you have inherited from your fathers," says Goethe, "you must earn for yourself before you can call it yours."

You will find plenty of people inside the churches and outside of them who are anxious to impose their philosophy upon you and your fellow men in the form of a creed. But the tendency of all such creeds is to become mere formulas. No creed or philosophy when thus imposed from outside is of much use to a growing man or a growing society in solving the problems which each change of circumstances necessarily brings. In order to be able to do this men must have brought the propositions of their creed into vital connection with their own experience of life.

There are two things that a man must

3

woo and win for himself: his bride and his philosophy. Mr. Huxley is said to have expressed the wish that he had some friend whose judgment he could trust to whom he could delegate the work of examining the claims of the Christian church upon a man's allegiance. He was anxious to know what should be his attitude toward that institution, and he was too busy with his work as a biologist to find the time for examination of the evidence. It will be remembered that Captain Miles Standish for somewhat similar reasons actually delegated to his friend John Alden the work of getting him a bride, he being too busy with the defense of the colony to have time for anything else. As matters fell out, however, Miles Standish was compelled to leave his bride to John Alden; and I suspect that if Huxley had really tried his experiment he would have ended by leaving his religion to his friend.

Some people acquire their philosophic views by actual contact with life itself; by meeting men of various types and temperaments and thus learning to look at the world's problems from different angles of vision. Others get the same result from books; they study the classics of literature and history and science, and find which things have proved large at all times instead of simply looking large for the moment. The college student has an opportunity of combining both these methods; and I count it one of the greatest privileges of college life to use this opportunity. In after years the man who goes into active business is cut off from contact with the past; the man who does not go into active business is cut off from contact with the present. To the college student more than to any one else it is given to feel the inspiration of old ideas and traditions and at the same time to discuss them with the men of today and by the methods of today. This affords him the opportunity for philosophic thought in the best and truest sense.

I shall not undertake in the brief compass of three lectures to furnish you with a ready-made philosophical system. If I did, and if I succeeded in condensing into three hours what might well fill three hundred, the resulting theories would be mine and not yours. All that I can do is to indicate some of the lines of thought in science, in politics, and in literature, which have met the needs of thinking men of successive generations in the nineteenth century.

Lines of thought, I say, in the plural, rather than line of thought, in the singular, because the nineteenth century has witnessed the development of a whole series of different philosophies—the positive philosophy of our grandfathers, the evolutionary philosophy of our fathers, and the so-called "pragmatist" philosophy which now appears to have displaced them both. We cannot speak of a nineteenth century fashion in thinking in the same way in which we speak of an eighteenth century fashion or a thirteenth century fashion. Fashions in thinking have changed nearly as fast as fashions in dress. System has succeeded system with bewildering frequency. The idol of today is the antiquarian curiosity of tomorrow. In my own student years and in those that immediately followed, philosophic interest centered about Herbert Spencer. Sometimes we agreed with him, sometimes we disagreed with him; but whether we agreed or disagreed, we were always intensely interested in what he said. His way of looking at the universe appealed to us, whether his specific theories did so or not. We were quite ready to admit that future

7

generations might modify his doctrines or might reject part of what he said; that future generations should cease to be interested in his philosophy and should say, "It may be true or it may not be true, but it is a rather uninteresting and useless kind of thing either way," never entered our minds. Yet this is precisely what has happened. The mode of thought which he represented has come and gone. Thirty years ago it was rather old-fashioned not to care for Herbert Spencer; today it is rather old-fashioned to care for him.

I shall not try to expound Herbert Spencer's philosophy or any of the other philosophies of the nineteenth century in detail. If you want to know what Spencer said you must read Spencer. If you want to know what Nietzsche said you must read Nietzsche. If you want to know what James said you must read James. Nor am I undertaking to decide which of

8

these philosophies is good and which is bad. Each philosophy was good so far as it met the needs of its own time. Each philosophy was bad so far as it failed to satisfy the wants of the next generation. What I wish to do is to go one step farther back—to show the concrete causes which led different groups of students and men of affairs to be interested in these successive philosophies one after another.

The wise historian does not generally attempt to decide which of his characters is noblest or which of their constitutional theories is the best. Plutarch tried this sort of thing now and then; but even in the case of Plutarch you will find that most of his comparisons of good men end by saying that each was good in his own way, and most of his comparisons of bad men end by saying that each was bad in his own way. "Tiberius had more virtues, but Agis had fewer faults"; so the comment runs, through the whole list. The real work of the historian is not so much to pass judgment on his characters as to explain the relation between these characters, good or bad, and the state of society which brought them to the front. He makes his chronicle of facts in one decade an explanation of the men of the next. I am going to try to do a little of the same sort of work for the history of nineteenth century philosophy. I shall try to tell as well as I can in so short a space some of the things that happened in the world of science and the world of politics which made people crave a different sort of explanation of the universe at the end of the century from that which satisfied most of them at the beginning. I hope by so doing to help some of you to understand more fully than you have done the real significance of these events, and to assist you in some slight degree in working out your own philosophy of life by setting forth some facts which have influenced the beliefs of thinking men of recent generations. In the words of one of the wisest Frenchmen of his age, Charles Dunoyer, *"Je n'impose rien, je ne propose même rien: j'expose."*

II

CHANGED CONCEPTIONS OF
SCIENCE

THE period from 1815 to 1848 lies intellectually very far removed from the present. The science and the literature, the politics and the ethics of our grandfathers were radically different from our own. We see the extent of the change when we contrast the poetry of Byron with that of Kipling, the music of Mendelssohn with that of Wagner, the essays of Sydney Smith with those of Chesterton, or the political philosophy of Malthus with that of Morley. The age that followed the French Revolution was more remote from the world of today than the age that preceded it. Macaulay—a most characteristic product of his time—is farther away

12

from us than Edmund Burke or Adam Smith.

If we try to find the common element in these illustrations I have cited, in order to construct for ourselves a picture of the feelings and habits of the time, the first thing we notice is a certain finality of statement and utterance. Lord Melbourne, a survival of an earlier period and the head of a ministry of which Macaulay was a brilliant member, once said with a sigh at the close of a cabinet meeting, "I only wish I were as sure of anything as young Tom Macaulay is of everything." I had in my hands a few months since a manuscript notebook of the first course of lectures on chemistry delivered by Professor Silliman at Yale College a century ago, after his return from a period of study with the great European masters. He said in substance: "Chemistry is to all intents and purposes a finished science. Whatever

13

may be done in the future, it is impossible that all ages to come, all put together, should ever make discoveries equal in number and importance to the things which have been found out in the last thirty or forty years." There is a similar utterance in Mill's Political Economy—all the more significant because Mill himself was one of the most modest of men in estimating his personal merits and achievements:

"Happily, there is nothing in the laws of Value which remains for the present or any future writer to clear up; the theory of the subject is complete: the only difficulty to be overcome is that of so stating it as to solve by anticipation the chief perplexities which occur in applying it: and to do this, some minuteness of exposition, and considerable demands on the patience of the reader, are unavoidable."

This spirit of finality carried with it a

14

good deal of intolerance. It is doubtful whether there was as much real liberty of thought in Europe in the first half of the nineteenth century as in the last half of the eighteenth. Physically, indeed, men were freer. There was less restriction of movement, less effort to circumscribe the emotions and dictate the actions of the people. But mentally, I suspect that men were less free—at any rate in the great centers of thought. It was harder rather than easier to do your thinking for yourself or to defy any of the manifold dictates of fashion. The eighteenth century had encouraged individuality of mind and of speech. It was fertile in novelties of every kind. The first half of the nineteenth century discouraged such individuality, whenever it seemed to threaten established social usages and conventions. The larger the man was, the more chance he had of achieving freedom in the eighteenth century; the larger the man was, the less chance he seemed to have of achieving freedom in the first half of the nineteenth. This was the age which killed Keats and ostracized Shelley; which shut up writers like Silvio Pellico in prison and drove philosophic thinkers like Marx into avowed antagonism to the social order.

A system of metaphysics which prevailed in England during that period illustrates the characteristics of the times. It is called the "common sense" philosophy. You are no longer to be compelled to believe what Aristotle tells you because Aristotle said it. You are no longer to be compelled to believe what the church tells you because the church says it. You are to believe what common sense tells you as *we* see it—"we" representing the respectable body of thinking men in the nineteenth century. You are at perfect liberty to believe otherwise; but if you do "we" shall perceive that you have no sense, and we shall treat you accordingly.

All this was natural enough. In the light of the political events which had immediately preceded, it was not only natural but inevitable. The ferment of eighteenth century thought, which had produced a Rousseau and a Voltaire, a Franklin and a Jefferson, a Goethe and a Napoleon, had also produced a revolution which had shaken the social order to its foundation and involved Europe in a series of wars unparalleled in their extent and severity. The world required rest. The need of progress was less conspicuous than the need of order. The need of free thought was less exigent than the need of coherent thought. The statesmen of Europe were trying to fit the broken pieces of European politics back into a monarchical scheme. The literary men of Europe were trying to substitute skilled treatment of safe themes for erratic treatment of unsafe ones. The period from 1815 to 1848 was, I think, an age of happiness and contentment for the majority of civilized people, because the majority of people were pretty well satisfied with the amount of liberty they themselves enjoyed, and did not mind very much if this or that man were denied a freedom for which they themselves felt no immediate craving. But it was not an age of progress, nor an age of liberty for progressively minded men.

From this state of intellectual complacency the world was gradually aroused by two somewhat independent sets of events—one in science, which will be described in this lecture, another in politics, which forms the theme of the next.

The science of the first half of the nineteenth century had been of an eminently safe character. It was at once correct and commonplace. People had abandoned the wilder ideas and hopes which had animated the investigators of earlier centuries. They no longer dabbled in the arts of magic or of prophecy. They no longer sought to transmute lead into gold, or to find the mysterious "elixir of life." Alchemy had given place to chemistry, astrology to astronomy. Investigators were not so much occupied with discovering principles as with ordering and arranging facts. The chemist had his list of elements, with the atomic weights which determined the proportions in which they combined; he had ceased to speculate on the nature of these atoms or to investigate with the interest that had animated his predecessors the strange processes which went on when different elements united. The physicist was content to describe and measure the phenomena of heat and sound and light and electricity; concerning the essential causes of these phenomena he was content to accept what Newton or Huyghens or Franklin had suggested. A single accident on the part of Benjamin Franklin in the choice of material for one of his electrical experiments was sufficient to give wrong shape to the whole form of electric theory for a century afterward. The geologist was more occupied with the description of his rocks and with the order in which they were probably deposited than with any investigation into the methods by which they had been produced. The botanist was satisfied to describe the plants that he saw and group them into classes according to their obvious resemblances. If, like Linnæus, he contented himself with arranging them according to superficial or accidental resemblances, the classification was called an artificial one. If, like DeCandolle, he tried to get at deeper and more essential characteristics as a basis of his system, the classification was said to be a natural one. But the object was the same in the two cases. You wanted to get your plant ticketed, so that the boy who counted its stamens or the man who dissected its pistils could know where to find it in the last edition of the encyclopædia if it was a well-known species, or where to put it in the next edition if it was a newly discovered one. The zoölogist had no profounder aim than the botanist. Even the human body was studied in the same purely descriptive spirit. Our knowledge was anatomical rather than physiological or pathological. Medical students were taught to describe its parts with accuracy; they were not taught with any corresponding degree of success to explain their development and their functions. The scientific instinct of that day was an impulse to name things and to identify them, rather than a craving to lay bare the hidden forces by which they were moved. We find this whole scheme of classification systematized and glorified in the positive philosophy of Auguste Comte, where the different branches of knowledge are themselves arranged in order and each science brought into what that philosopher believed to be a proper relation to other sciences as part of an articulated whole.

The middle of the nineteenth century witnessed the development of three great discoveries which aroused the world from this intellectual complacency, changed the character of modern science, and emboldened people to try to explain things which they had previously been content to describe and arrange. These were the law of the conservation of energy, the theory of cellular tissue, and the process of elimination by natural selection.

The doctrine of the conservation of energy was the first of the three to be fully developed.

The physicists of a hundred years ago—or natural philosophers, as they would then have called themselves—described the behavior of a number of phenomena like heat and sound and light, which they treated as independent things. The chemists of the same period described and classified separate elements, and ridiculed the efforts of the earlier alchemists to find some force which might possibly transmute one element into another. There had been, indeed, a few brilliant thinkers, like our own fellow countryman, Count Rumford, who had suggested that these different things might not be so wholly independent as they seemed. But such men were isolated, and their voices were unheard or forgotten.

About 1840 two physicians, studying

separately, one in Hamburg and another
in Manchester, developed a theory that
heat was a form of manifestation of
motion; that mechanics and thermodynamics, instead of being separate
sciences, were one and the same science;
that the combustion of the coal in the fur-
nace and the expansion of the steam in
the boiler represented simply the trans-
mutations of energy from one form into
another; and that each unit of heat had
its mechanical equivalent in terms of
motion. The researches of Dr. Mayer
and Dr. Joule were carried further by a
line of eminent observers and mathema-
ticians—Faraday, Tyndall, Helmholtz,
and a score of others whose names
are household words today. Sound and
light, as well as heat, were found to be
manifestations of this same transmutable
energy in another form. Electrical phenomena were explained in the same

24

manner. The whole modern system of electrical engineering has been based upon mechanical laws, more complex indeed than those of thermodynamics but apparently not less sure. Even chemical action and chemical combination have been treated as being manifestations of energy in still another form; energy which is stored up at one time or under one set of conditions, and becomes "potentially" available to be set free in another. The chemist is no longer content when he has weighed his substances or measured the volumes of his gases; but he strives with ever increasing success to coördinate all chemical phenomena under a few basic laws.

A somewhat similar change was wrought in biological science by the development of the theory of cellular tissue.

It was not a wholly new idea that living bodies were composed of a multitude of small cells, each with an independent activity of its own. Caspar Wolff in Germany and Bichat in France had enunciated doctrines of this kind in the eighteenth century. But it was reserved for the nineteenth century to show how the study of the behavior of these cells could explain the life history of the plants and animals in which they were gathered together. Schwann at Berlin, in the years from 1834 to 1838, first emphasized the possible importance of this method of explanation. The views of Schwann had to be modified in many essential respects; but they formed a basis for the theory of cellular tissue or protoplasm developed by DuBois-Reymond and Huxley and Virchow, which wrought a change in the whole underlying conception and purpose of the biological sciences similar to that which the doctrine of conservation of energy had wrought in the physical sciences. These sciences ceased to be merely descriptive; they became in a fuller sense explanatory. They looked less at the outside of things and more at the inside. Morphology gave place to physiology. The museum counted for less as an instrument of the scientist's study, the laboratory for more. The biologist was no longer content to describe the anatomy of plants and animals and men; he wanted to know their life history. It was not enough to classify them by their external forms or to explain the functions of the different parts; he must know how they grow and become strong or why they become weak and die. Our books of botany and zoölogy have become something more than well-ordered indexes of the different forms of plant and animal life. They occupy themselves with the processes of fertilization and nutrition and differentiation of activity on the one hand, or of disease and death on the other.

But these two discoveries, wide reaching as they were, affected chiefly the thoughts and processes of the professional student of science. The third great discovery, of the principle of natural selection, wrought a similar transformation in the thoughts of the world as a whole.

People sometimes speak of natural selection and evolution as though they were the same thing. This is not true. The idea of evolution is old. The idea of the establishment of types and species by natural selection is surprisingly new. The importance of the process of natural selection was discovered and its methods of operation were developed simultaneously and to a large extent independently by Charles Darwin and Alfred Russel Wallace about the middle of the nineteenth century. The botanist or zoölogist of a generation previous had been content to describe the fern or the rose, the oyster or the rabbit. The cell theory enabled him to go one step farther, and to explain the life history of each of these types of organism. But it did not help him to account for the types themselves; it did not show why there were ferns and why there were roses, why there were oysters and why there were rabbits. Darwinism offered a solution of this problem. Darwin taught that each type or species was developed by a gradual process of adaptation to its surroundings through a long series of generations. He explained the life history of the type as well as the life history of the individual.

No two living creatures are exactly alike. Both among plants and among animals the offspring varies slightly from the parent stock. Some of these variations tend to preserve the life of the plant or animal in its struggle for existence, others tend to hinder it. The characteristics that prove a hindrance in the struggle are eliminated by the death of the individuals that possess them. The characteristics that prove a help in the struggle are preserved. It is immaterial whether the advantageous trait which at first sprung up by accident be communicated by inheritance or whether it become universal by the slower process of eliminating all the individuals that do not possess it. The result is the same in either case.

Such was Darwin's theory of natural selection. In spite of the patience with which it had been developed and the brilliant reasoning with which it was urged, many of Darwin's contemporaries hesitated to accept it because it undertook to explain so much which previous generations had been compelled to take for granted. But the younger men received it with enthusiasm; and each decade as it has passed has confirmed the essential correctness of Darwin's conclusions. The evidence furnished by the progress of geological science was particularly strong. The successive series of fossil-bearing strata showed a development and differentiation of the forms of animal and plant life which indicated that different species were not created all at once or by separate acts of miraculous power, but by an orderly process of elimination and survival.

The influence of Darwin in modifying scientific conceptions did not stop with animal and vegetable physiology. It soon became evident that the principle of natural selection would explain more things and more important things than the origin of biological species. Human life, even more than plant life or animal life, represents a constant series of variations. The whole process of history as we see it going on about us is a record of a struggle for existence. Those who are adapted to their surroundings maintain their place in line; those who are ill adapted fall by the wayside. It is by a process like this that tribes and nations are welded together; it is·by a process like this that political institutions are built up. In a book like Bagehot's *Physics and Politics* we see traced out the application of Darwin's theory and the explanation of the public life of organized bodies of men. In fact, the application of the Darwinian theory to political history is clearer than its application to natural history, and its successive steps can be traced far more surely.

Nor does the application of the theory stop short with politics. It explains the origin and development of ethical conceptions as no other theory has ever yet been able to explain them. The human struggle for existence is not a struggle between individuals. It is a struggle between groups, in which the morals of the group

count for more than the physical characteristics of the individual members. Looking back over the record of human history
as far as we can trace it, we see that the
savage was gradually crowded out by the
civilized man because the civilized man had
developed discipline and sympathy and
toleration; because he had learned to substitute reverence for superstition and
true fortitude for mere animal courage;
because he had accustomed himself to keep
his temper and to put the law above personal interests, and to live in charity with
a larger and larger section of mankind.
The whole progress of civilization, so far
as it is worth recording, is the record of
the displacement of animal excellences by
human ones and of savage virtues by
civilized ones. This displacement follows
the lines laid down by Darwin in his
theories of animal and plant life; and it is
being understood and developed today as

it could not have been understood and developed two generations ago.

It will perhaps seem strange to some of you if I say that Darwinism has become the basis of a new spiritual philosophy of life. Yet this statement is profoundly true; and its truth becomes more obvious the more we compare the old science and the old scientific thinking with the new. The positive philosophy of Comte, to which I have already alluded, represented a view of life and thought which was widely current in the early half of the century. Comte's philosophy was distinctly anti-spiritual. He said that science in its progress toward perfection went through three stages: the theological stage, where everything was explained by the action of God; the metaphysical stage, where people tried to explain things by theories; and the truly scientific stage, where they were content to look at facts. Comte's ideal of

perfect science was a beautifully ordered
index of the universe, where God was
entirely left out and where law meant little
more than classification. The Darwinian
theory has reintroduced ideas of law which
Comte would have characterized as metaphysical, and has made room for ideas of
God which Comte would have contemned
as theological. The scientific man today
is concerned to find the purpose and reason
of things. He is concerned to bring the
individual facts, not only into their proper
place in a scheme of the universe, but into
their proper subordination to a series of
forces which he figures and conceives in
terms at which Comte would have shud-
dered. He is concerned to study the right
and wrong of things; and he believes, as
the very essence of his theory, that the
right is that which will prevail in the long
run. The philosophy of the Darwinian is
in its essence the philosophy of Gamaliel:

"If this counsel or this work be of men, it will come to nought: but if it be of God, ye cannot overthrow it; lest haply ye be found even to fight against God."

To the man who, like the founder of these lectures, finds in an ordered universe an evidence of a wise creator and a revelation of God's methods, the Darwinian theory comes as a welcome contribution of science to theistic philosophy. It was unfortunately not received in that spirit by the world as a whole. Men who had been brought up to think that God created the world in one way, however irrational and disorderly, believed that his worship was threatened by any evidence that went to show that it had been created in some other way, however rational and orderly. In this respect, the Darwinian theory has simply suffered the fate which has at first befallen every scientific discovery which was stated in terms that the public could understand. When Copernicus and Galileo developed the theory that the earth and all the other planets moved round the sun, they gave us an orderly and simple astronomical system instead of a disorderly and complicated one; yet the Copernican system was condemned by conservative men as impious, because they had been brought up to believe that God had made the world in a different way and they could find scripture texts which seemed to support their position. We have learned better. We have found out that God's rulership of the universe is not dependent upon the relative positions of the earth and the sun in our planetary system; and we leave it to men like John Jasper to make it a fundamental doctrine of the church that "the sun do move." But not all churches have yet learned to treat the principle of natural selection in the same large-minded spirit. Men of standing and influence in the community condemned the theory that species had been created under the operation of general laws, in the same way and for nearly the same reason that their ancestors two centuries earlier had condemned the doctrine that the earth and the other planets moved around the sun under the operation of general laws.

Nor was this kind of misunderstanding confined to the opponents of the Darwinian theory. Many of those who supposed that they were advocating it enthusiastically preached it in forms which its founder would hardly have recognized and based its advocacy on reasons which he would have repudiated. "There is a picture of Charles Darwin in thousands of homes," said a careful student of social problems, "whose occupants care nothing for science and know nothing of what Darwin really said, but who revere him because he is an intellectual force on which their priests have declared war. They love him, not for the order that he has introduced into our thinking, but for the disorder which he has been falsely charged with introducing." For one man who knows Darwin at first hand—careful, peaceful, and slow to generalize—there are twenty who identify him with the diatribes of Haeckel or the metaphysical theories of Herbert Spencer.

We shall best understand the true significance of Darwinism if we dissociate it from the polemics which have been waged about it and the philosophies which have connected themselves with it, and treat it for what it was—an orderly explanation of facts which previously had not been explained; the last, and in many respects the most novel, of the three great theoretical discoveries which the nineteenth century has contributed to the development of modern science.

III

NEW VIEWS OF POLITICS AND OF ETHICS

THE political thought of Europe since 1789 has passed through three phases or stages: the revolutionary stage from 1789 to 1815, the individualistic stage from 1815 to 1848, and the nationalistic stage from 1848 onward.

The ideals of the revolutionary thinkers were summed up in the three watchwords, Liberty, Equality, and Fraternity. These were not mere phrases, as some people are inclined to assume. They represented important political ideals and aspirations. But none of these watchwords meant quite what we are apt to think it did. The Frenchmen of 1789 did not understand the term liberty as an American or Englishman understands it. They did not mean the right of each man to mind his own business, or what he regarded as his own business; they meant the right of every man to mind other people's business. They meant by liberty much more nearly what we now mean by democracy. They wanted to put the government directly into the hands of the voters, with as few limitations as possible upon popular action. Liberty, in their minds, was not only opposed to monarchy, which put the government in the hands of a sovereign; but it was almost equally opposed to constitution-alism, which compelled the government to proceed deliberately and to exercise its power within traditional limits and by traditional methods.

Nor did they understand the term equality as meaning communism, though some of the leaders of the French Revolu-. tion in its later stages were themselves communists. They did not intend to abolish property. They did not even intend to abolish all inequalities of ownership or condition. Equality meant government under general laws that applied to all people alike, as distinct from the system of privilege or class legislation that had prevailed in France up to the close of the last century—with one law for the noble, another for the priest, another for the merchant, and another for the farmer.

Nor did the term fraternity mean the practical exercise of brotherly love. It meant an aspiration toward harmony of interests among different members of the human race instead of the *bellum omnium contra omnes* which earlier philosophers had assumed to be the natural and normal state. When the French Revolutionists added the word fraternity to the words liberty and equality, they meant that by putting government in the hands of the people and governing under general laws, they expected to govern for the good of humanity as a whole. Fraternity was opposed to intellectual selfishness, whether individual or national.

The French Revolution came and went. After a quarter of a century of struggle the first of the objects of the Revolutionists—liberty as its champions conceived it—remained unrealized. The second and third objects, equality and fraternity, were secured to a substantial degree.

The experiment of putting unrestricted power into the hands of the people had failed. Pure or unconstitutional democracy had worked so badly that it wrought its own ruin. France and Germany had gone back to the hands of the old monarchical families. But equality—government of the people under general laws—had worked well. The communities that enjoyed its benefits increased rapidly in prosperity and in intelligence. Prior to 1789

England and America had been the only countries where the general principles of the law applied indiscriminately to everybody, instead of applying in one way to the noble and in another way to the peasant. The result was that the standard of life of the people in England and America had been much better than in France or Germany. When the system of equality was applied to France the general condition of the French people was quick to improve. When the same thing was applied to western Germany, even though it was imposed by a foreign hand, western Germany responded in the same fashion. The Napoleonic code gave it better government than it had ever had before. The people became accustomed to look at law as a thing to be applied impartially to all individuals, instead of differently for different classes. Down to the present day there is a contrast in the public attitude on this matter between those parts of Germany where the code prevailed and those where it did not.

In a remarkable letter to his brother, Napoleon said that the sentiment which would result from this kind of government would be a strong barrier against the attempt of states like Prussia and Austria to reconquer western Germany. His prevision was fulfilled, though in a different manner from what he expected. The code did not prevent Prussia and Austria from returning into power in the German Confederation; but it did prevent them from exercising that power to put things back where they were before. The petty princes in Germany were no more able to abolish the principle of equality than were the Bourbons in France. They would have been glad to do so, for they hated it with all their hearts; but it was beyond their power. Napoleon's military successes had been followed by defeat. His legal success in establishing the code that bears his name was more permanent, and gives him, I think, a firmer title to fame than did his military victories. The Bourbons could overthrow democracy, because democracy had worked badly. They could not overthrow equality, because equality had worked well.

Nor did they overthrow the aspirations and aims which were embodied in the term fraternity. In fact, they tried to annex them and use them for their own purposes. The sovereigns who formed the Holy Alliance during the years from 1815 to 1825 claimed to be serving the sacred cause of humanity when they persecuted republicans, just as glibly as did the Committee of Public Safety when they persecuted Royalists a generation earlier; and in each case it is probable that many of the perpetrators of deeds of violence honestly believed that they were doing it for the good of all mankind. Alexander of Russia and St. Just of the Terror had more in common than either of them would have liked to admit. What was true to some degree of monarchs was true to an even larger degree of political and literary leaders. Enthusiasm for the human race as a whole was fashionable. The religion of humanity became a watchword. The statement of the utilitarians that moral and political good meant neither more nor less than the greatest happiness of the greatest number, was accepted as an axiom or postulate of ethical science.

Taking the principle of equality before the law as a starting point, and the attainment of the greatest happiness of the greatest number as a goal, Jeremy Bentham and his followers developed the system of political philosophy known as individualism. Bentham's *Fragment on Government,* like Adam Smith's *Wealth of Nations,* appeared in 1776; but the full working out of his theories was reserved for the century following, when a succession of brilliant English and French writers, beginning with Ricardo and ending with John Stuart Mill, undertook to make them the basis of social order and social progress.

The underlying idea of individualism is that the free action of intelligent men, working out their own ideas independently, will produce a good collective result for the community. The individualist is essentially an optimist. He believes that enlightened selfishness tends to make a man do well for others besides himself, and that the work of the law maker consists chiefly in giving each man a fair chance to pursue his own ends with as much enlightenment and as little interference as possible. The statement which is frequently made that individualism regards humanity as made up of disconnected and warring atoms—I quote this from an address by the Bishop of Durham twenty-five years ago—is precisely the reverse of the truth. The individualist believes that men naturally work together instead of apart; and his mistakes, such as they are, arise from exaggerating the harmony of human interests instead of underrating it.

I have spoken of individualism as dating from Ricardo and Bentham. But its origin is really to be sought in the decisions of the English common law judges during the three or four centuries that had preceded. These judges discovered the principle of competition and the beneficent results that competition would produce. They saw that if a baker charged too high a price for his bread, the thing to do was to encourage other bakers to come into the

49

same community and increase the supply. The self-interest of the bakers would produce better results than the punitive action of the magistrates. Of course there were exceptions which had to be dealt with by exceptional methods. There were times when the high price of bread was the result of a conspiracy, and then it was right to punish the conspirators. But in nine cases out of ten the high price was the symptom of scarcity; and the best way of dealing with the evil was to make it for the interest of other people to come and lower the price by the only method that was permanently effectual—by the offer of additional supplies. When a man finds the best market for his own goods he is generally rendering the maximum service to other men.

But though the English judges apprehended and stated this principle clearly, they were far from appreciating how

widely it could be applied. They used it
as a means of justifying certain methods
of price regulation and rejecting certain
other methods. It was not until the latter
part of the eighteenth century that Adam
Smith showed how this principle could be
made the basis, not merely for deciding a
few judicial controversies, but for explain-
ing the causes that determine the wealth
of nations. It was not until the generation
after Adam Smith that it became the
foundation of an organized system of
political economy, as developed by Ricardo
and Malthus and their associates. Principles which had been buried for centuries
in law books and law reports now became
matter of common interest, because the
time was ripe for their acceptance. The
public mind of that generation welcomed
the theory that free competition among
individuals and free trade among nations
represented the normal condition of busi-

ness activity, and that any interference with this condition was at best an unfortunate necessity.. Nor was the application of these theories confined to the field of economics. Herbert Spencer, in one of his earlier works, his *Social Statics,* tried to show how the exercise of individual intelligence would produce the same kind of results in politics and in morals that it did in business. "The best government is that which governs least"—this was a phrase so often repeated that it became a proverb and took its place in the book of current phrases, along with that similar mixture of wisdom and unwisdom, "Happy is the nation that has no history."

To people who look at politics and morals in this way, the actual form of government may become a matter of relatively little concern. The less the sovereign does the less does it matter who is sovereign. If the citizens are to be allowed to direct their own affairs as much as possible, it is of comparatively little consequence whether the government is elective or hereditary, democratic or aristocratic.

For a long time the individualists had everything their own way. The monopolies and privileges granted in the eighteenth century had been so bad that their removal did much good and little harm. The restrictions upon trade in different communities had been so arbitrary that the removal of these restrictions tended to increase prosperity in at least nine cases out of ten. The liberty which people sought in the days following the downfall of Napoleon was the English kind of liberty rather than the French kind of liberty—freedom to pursue one's own course with as little interference from 'others as possible, rather than freedom to hold frequent elections in order that the

majority of men might decide what the
minority should be compelled to do. For
a long time the voice of Hegel was the
only important one that was lifted in protest. But as early as 1830 symptoms of a
somewhat widespread reaction in thought
began to make themselves manifest—
reaction against individualism and in favor
of socialism. It is rather interesting to
note that the word "socialism" was coined
to designate, not so much a positive theory
or programme, as a protest against individualism and its consequences; to express
by a single phrase the attitude of those
who did not believe that the needs of the
community could be met by the independent action of its individual members.

The first attacks of the socialists were
not directed against the general principle
that free play of individual activity would
produce the best results for the community, but against the idea that there could

be, under existing legal conditions, anything like free play of individual activity.
There is not equality of opportunity, said
Marx; and any results which are predi-
cated upon an alleged equality of opportunity for all men must be false results.
Theoretically you expect all to share alike
in the benefits of competition. Practically
it may mean the exploitation of the weak
by the strong. Theoretically you say that
every one has a fair chance at the gains of
industrial enterprise. Practically the man
who has gotten hold of capital, whether
by good fortune, by inheritance, or by ras-
cality, has an advantage which it is hard
for any one else to overcome. It is only
too easy to find cases where the laborers
have been in fact exploited; cases where
the freest opportunity to trade has produced inequality instead of equality. By a
skilful citation and presentation of these
cases, the socialists excited the laborers of

European cities to a ferment which culminated in the Revolution of 1848.

The immediate effect of this Revolution was to bring radical leaders to the front and give them a chance to try their theories. The result of this trial was not successful. A few months' experiment with the practical workings of socialism dealt the cause a blow from which it took it at least a generation to recover. However good the theories of Marx might sound, the practical application of them was disastrous. But in spite of this failure and the resulting discredit of socialism, people did not go back to the old ideas of free trade and enthusiasm for the cause of humanity. National aspirations had been awakened by the Revolution; national feelings and sentiments came into play. Though the efforts of Hungary and of Italy in 1849 were crushed, the spirit which they engendered remained and grew

strong. Italy became a nation in 1859;
the United States, in 1865; Germany, in
1866. Russia proclaimed herself the
champion of Slavonic unity, and in 1878
succeeded in freeing the peoples of the
lower Danube from the domination of
Turkey. The sentiment of patriotism
grew; the sentiment of humanitarianism
was forced into the background. The man
who was an intense patriot found it hard
to be devoted to the religion of humanity.
A good American cared more for his fellow Americans than he did for those who
had been unfortunate enough to be born in
England or France or Germany and be-
nighted enough to remain there. It was
the same way with other countries. "The
whole Eastern question is not worth the
blood of a single soldier from the German
fatherland," was the remark of no less a
person than Bismarck himself, the greatest
leader in all this nationalistic movement.

In the years which followed the Revolution of 1848, a large part of the socialistic sentiment turned itself into the new "nationalistic" channels opened for it by men like Bismarck and Cavour. While Marx was vainly striving to keep the "International" together, Ferdinand Lassalle and his followers welcomed the growth of national government as a means of curbing the power of industrial organizations. Bismarck wanted to strengthen the king of Prussia; Lassalle wanted to weaken the bankers in Frankfort. For the moment the interests of the two coincided. I shall not attempt to trace in detail the history of the nationalistic movement which changed loose federations of states to strong centralized governments, and produced successively a united Italy, a united America, and a united Germany. I shall simply call your attention to its effect in producing two industrial conse-

quences of great importance, high tariffs
and large standing armies—or, if you prefer to express the change in abstract terms
instead of concrete ones, protection and
militarism.

Down to 1860 Europe had moved gradually but surely in the direction of free
trade. Tariffs were lowered; international
exchange of products was encouraged by
the statesmen of the several countries. It
was held that if different nations had
advantages for producing different sets of
goods, the gain by trade was mutual; in
short, that division of labor between
nations was as natural and normal a thing
as division of labor between individuals.
With the advent of the nationalistic spirit
there arose a desire on the part of each
people to be sufficient for itself; a feeling
that trade with other nations meant de-
pendence upon other nations; a suspicion
that the gain in foreign commerce was not

a mutual advantage but an advantage that accrued to the one that exported most goods and got most gold in return. Tariffs began to go up instead of to go down. Taxes imposed temporarily as war measures were retained after the wars themselves had ceased.

In like manner the standing armies which nations had supported during the early part of the nineteenth century were relatively small. Even those countries like Germany or Austria, which had a large and officious internal police, maintained comparatively small military establishments for defense against their neighbors. The years following 1860 witnessed a change in this respect also. The system of compulsory military service for the whole body of grown men was enforced by Bismarck and Moltke, until it was possible to convert the nation into an armed camp on a few days' notice. The successes

of Prussia against Austria in 1866 and
France in 1870 caused the other nations
of the European continent to model their
establishments upon that of Prussia. The
desire of different peoples to have colonies
in which to make money, and world-wide
possessions to give an imperial character
to their dominion, led to an increase in
the world's navies proportionate to that
which had already come about in the
world's armies. So definite is the popular
conviction of the necessity of these military establishments and so profound the
distrust that each nation feels concerning
the intentions of its neighbors, that the
proposal made at the beginning of the
first Hague Conference to reduce by
mutual agreement the armed forces of the
powers represented was definitively re-
jected and came near wrecking the success
of the conference as a whole.

We no longer assume that the interests

of nations are identical. We no longer
assume that it is desirable to remove bar-
riers that separate humanity into different
parts. We have pretty much abolished
"fraternity." We are so full of national
aspirations that human aspirations fall
into the background. Each nation wants
to be the strongest. If a change in the
tariff law hurts England or Germany, we
think that it is probably good for America.
In place of a well-ordered harmony of
interests, which the statesmen of 1850
tried in their various ways to compass, the
statesmen of 1900 content themselves with
some semblance of order in their antag-
onisms.

This change of feeling about politics and
about trade was accompanied by a similar
change of feeling about morals.

Down to the middle of the century
there had been a tendency to assume that

the interests of the individual and the interests of the community were identical, and that any seeming antagonism between the two was due to want of intelligence. Rational selfishness and rational unselfishness were thought to lead to identical results. If you could only teach a man to know what was really good for him he would do what was good for the community, and be rewarded by permanent prosperity and by the approval of his fellow men, instead of doing what he thought good for himself and getting his reward in the shape of pleasures of a lower or less lasting character. This was a comfortable theory to hold. If you believed people were going to be selfish in any event, it was pleasant to think that their selfishness would have good results for others. If you were anxious to have the community prosperous, it was pleasant to think that this end could be secured by appeals to individual self-interest no less than to individual public spirit. But there were so many cases where things did not work that way—where selfishness went without punishment and unselfishness without reward—that this theory of harmony of interests was abandoned. Some men, like Carlyle, boldly attacked liberty and proclaimed themselves champions of authority. The necessary and desirable thing for a nation, according to Carlyle, was not to let each man take his own way, but to let all men unite in obeying the strongest and best. Those who continued to defend liberty did so, not because the free action of the individual necessarily produced the best results for the community, but because it gave people the best chance of finding who was fitted to lead.

In England, the break between the old and the new liberalism was not a sharp or sudden one. The English liberals, under the leadership of John Stuart Mill, gradually and almost insensibly gave up the belief that individual selfishness would produce the best results for the community, and substituted the doctrine that individual freedom would allow the community to watch the results of different experiments to see which it should stamp with its approval. John Morley, the best exponent of this new school of thought, says with justice, that Carlyle and his followers appealed to men to follow the hero, but never gave any directions how to find him; while Mill's doctrine laid down the main conditions of finding your hero, namely: that all roads should be left open to him, because no living man knew by which road he would come.

While the discussion was thus waged in England between men like Carlyle and Ruskin on the one side, and Mill and Morley on the other, a school of thinkers on the Continent had grappled with the question in their own fashion and given a bolder, though not a sounder, answer. Rational conduct, they said, was necessarily calculated selfishness. If this selfishness of the individual would not work out benefits for the community as a whole, so much the worse for the community. Life, in the view of these men, is a struggle between many types of men, in which each individual strives to develop his powers and make his will the dominant one. The best man is the one who succeeds.

Friedrich Nietzsche is commonly regarded as the leader of this school, which, among the many perversions of Darwinism, is perhaps the most perverse. But Nietzsche himself was a writer of aphorisms rather than a framer of systems. For a connected statement of the results of his thinking we must look rather to the work of his followers. Take, for instance, the book of Loria, on *The Economic Foundations of the Constitution of Society.* Right, says Loria, is a mere convention— what each nation chooses to make it. A few men get hold of authority; they make rules to benefit themselves at the expense of other members of society. If these rules are simply laws and nothing more, it is necessary to have police to enforce them. Police are very expensive; and moreover the police, like the Turkish janizaries, may take it into their heads to enforce the laws against you instead of against somebody else. It is therefore more convenient and effective to do away with the necessity for so many police, by persuading the people that these laws have supernatural sanction and that the gods will punish them if the police do not. This, they say, is the origin and real nature of morality. Let the enlightened man emancipate himself from these delusions. Let him see that law is a convention and morality a superstition. Let him realize to the utmost his own individual purposes and individual aims. Play the game for yourself:—this, says the follower of Nietzsche, is the only rational theory of conduct, this the only philosophic view of life.

This sounds like dangerous advice. So it is—for the man that follows it. A high-minded philosopher of this school, like Nietzsche himself, becomes insane; a low-minded philosopher of this school, like D'Annunzio, falls into animalism. If the current system of morality be an illusion, it is at any rate an illusion that protects the man and the race that hold it. If the rejection of tradition and rule in the effort to play the game for one's self be enlightenment, it is the enlightenment that leads to the ditch on the one hand or the quagmire on the other. Whatever may be the errors or the dangers in the complacent optimism of English philosophers, they have proved infinitely less destructive than the complacent, not to say brutal, pessimism of their brethren on the Continent.

Both these modes of thought appear to be giving place to a new philosophy, or perhaps I should rather say, to a new view of life, known by the somewhat unfortunate name of pragmatism. Of this philosophy, which is essentially a development of John Morley's theory of toleration, William James was the first popular advocate. Henri Bergson of Paris is today its best recognized exponent. In spite of all that these eminent writers have done, the most compact and useful statement of the principles of pragmatism is found in the fifth chapter of the Acts of the Apostles. I am not now referring to the early part of the chapter, that treats of the doings of a man named Ananias; but to the latter part, from which I made a brief quotation in the previous lecture, giving the counsel of a wiser man named Gamaliel, a doctor of the law, who said concerning the apostles:

"Ye men of Israel, take heed to yourselves what ye intend to do as touching these men.

"For before these days rose up Theudas, boasting himself to be somebody; to whom a number of men, about four hundred, joined themselves: who was slain; and all, as many as obeyed him, were scattered, and brought to nought.

"After this man rose up Judas of Galilee in the days of the taxing, and drew away much people after him: he also perished; and all, even as many as obeyed him, were dispersed.

"And now I say unto you, Refrain from these men, and let them alone: for if this counsel or this work be of men, it will come to nought:

"But if it be of God, ye cannot over-throw it; lest haply ye be found even to fight against God."

The criterion which shows whether a thing is right or wrong is its permanence. Survival is not merely the characteristic of right; it is the test of right. This is what distinguishes the philosophy of the prag-matist from that of Herbert Spencer. Her-bert Spencer made up his mind what he thought was right, and then tried to prove that the universe was working in that direction. The pragmatist tries to find, with as little prejudice as possible, the direction in which the universe is work-ing; and he makes that the criterion of right. Spencer was fundamentally a meta-physician. Although he had a prodigious knowledge of fact, he was constantly try-ing to arrange the facts to fit his theories. The philosopher of today, even when he is using the same terms, is concerned rather to make his theories fit the facts. He may not always succeed, but in method and purpose he has a fundamental advantage over the evolutionist of the generation that preceded him.

In the lower forms of animal life, where the struggle is between individuals, the plant or the animal that survives is the one we call best, because it is best adapted to its purpose. As we come higher up in the scale the struggle is no longer between individuals but between families, between groups, and ultimately between different systems of ethics. It is no longer the most perfectly developed individual, but the most perfectly organized group or the most perfectly harmonized system that prevails and thereby proves its right to prevail. It is here that the pragmatist takes issue with Nietzsche and his followers. The struggle between individuals within the group, though not entirely abolished, is and must be subordinated to the discipline of the group and the rules of the aspirations of the group, lest all perish together. We hold the beliefs which have preserved our fathers. It is not far from the truth to say that we hold them because they have preserved our fathers. I do not mean that we should consciously adopt a belief because it is useful to us, as James seems to imply. I would rather take the ground that we hold the belief that has preserved our fathers as an intuition and act on it as an instinct. The surest knowledge, according to the pragmatist, is that which has been thus established by the habit of generations until it becomes intuitive. Reasoning is of the nature of exploration. If we have to reason, it means that there is an absence of consensus of opinion among our fellows, and probably an absence of certainty in our own minds. I think it possible that

every thoroughgoing pragmatist ten years
hence will say that what we know we know
by instinct, and the use of the intellect is a
confession of ignorance. This much at
least is certain: that the better we know
how to do a thing, the less do we have to
make conscious use of our reasoning in
doing it.

What then is the bearing of all this
psychology on political and moral philosophy? To bring us back to the fundamental truth that we are members one of
another. Society is not a mere aggrega-
tion of individuals bound together by ties
of self-interest, as philosophers would
have told us in the first half of the nineteenth century; still less is it an aggrega-
tion of individuals set apart from one
another by the struggle for existence, as
some men were telling us twenty-five years
ago. Human history represents a struggle
of groups rather than a struggle of sepa-

rate men and women. The moral and religious instincts that bind the group together, which some men, not so many years ago, were condemning as outworn prejudices, count for even more than the individual intelligence. In our practical philosophy, of politics and of life, we are reverting to the words of Edmund Burke:

"We are afraid to put men to live and trade each on his own private stock of reason, because we suspect that this stock in each man is small, and that the individuals would do better to avail themselves of the general bank and capital of nations and of ages. Many of our men of speculation, instead of exploding general prejudices, employ their sagacity to discover the latent wisdom which prevails in them. If they find what they seek, and they seldom fail, they think it more wise to continue the prejudice with the reason involved, than to cast away the coat of prejudice, and to leave nothing but the naked reason: because prejudice with its reason has a motive to give action to that reason, and an affection which will give it permanence. . . . . Prejudice renders a man's virtue his habit, and not a series of unconnected acts. Through just prejudice, his duty becomes a part of his nature."

IV

THE SPIRITUAL BASIS OF RECENT POETRY

THE world changes the modes of its religious feeling and thought as it changes the modes of its political feeling and thought. The two sets of changes go hand in hand. An age of political complacence is usually an age of religious complacence. An age of political struggle is almost always an age of religious struggle. We think of the Reformation as a religious movement, and we think of the French Revolution as a political movement; but the Reformation was a time of political upheavals no less than of religious ones, and the French Revolution was marked by just as profound convulsions in the world of religion as in the world of politics.

In the ages of peace, when authority is accepted as a matter of course, the religious element in literature is apt to be essentially mystical—a confession of human weakness, an expression of human aspirations, a devout homage from a man who feels himself weak to a God who is immeasurably above him. In the ages of conflict and upheaval religious literature takes a different character. The time no longer calls for meditation, but for fighting—for fighting in which each man's own individual work may be overwhelmingly important. The sense of humility gives place to the feeling of responsibility; the vagueness of the aspiration to be like God gives place to the assertion of the overwhelming importance of bringing God and the world together. The peaceful devotion of the psalmist is overborne by the convulsive struggles of the prophet. The quiet of the gods is invaded by the cries of humanity. Their very authority is challenged by the indomitable will of Prometheus, the friend of man. In such an age it is no longer to the voice of David, but to that of Ezekiel, that we respond. It is no longer the song of Hesiod or even of Pindar, but the song of Aeschylus and of Euripides, that moves men.

A single instance, chosen to illustrate this contrast, will show what I mean better than any amount of description.

In a passage of *In Memoriam,* much admired at the time of its publication and still much quoted, Tennyson voiced the religious thought of a large part of the English-speaking world of his day in the following lines:

> " So runs my dream: but what am I?
> An infant crying in the night:
> An infant crying for the light:
> And with no language but a cry."

Not quite fifty years later another poet,

Henley, less known to the casual reader but not less significant in the history of English literature, put these burning words on paper:

> " Out of the night that covers me,
>   Black as the Pit from pole to pole,
> I thank whatever gods may be
>   For my unconquerable soul."

In time these two utterances are less than half a century apart; in spirit fifty centuries would not measure the difference.

The first half of the nineteenth century was an age of religious peace—an age when church authority was accepted as a fact, whether the people believed in the doctrines of the church or not. Their doubt and disbelief were essentially intellectual things which did not greatly affect their outward conduct or even their inward feelings. The ideal and the aim of those who put their religious emotions into poetry was quiet submission to the authority of God. They were content to accept as mysteries the things that they could not understand, and by this acceptance to achieve in their own souls the peace of God that passeth understanding. The second half of the century was an age of religious effort, of struggle. The religious poetry of the time, and a great deal that was not avowedly religious, was concerned with finding man's place in that struggle. The God of the later days was one who had come not to send peace but a sword; the true man of the later days was the one who tried unflinchingly to do his part, who never shrank from the conflict because he could not see the end. To accept the burdens and the mistakes of conflict rather than seek refuge in the quiet haven of mysticism—this is the message of the last years of the nineteenth century.

No longer do we content ourselves with saying, as Tennyson did:

"Our wills are ours, we know not how;
Our wills are ours, to make them thine."

We deem it a truer, as well as a nobler conception of life, to say with the more modern poet:

"East and west and north, wherever the battle grew,
Forth to a feast we fared, the work of the will to do.
Pillar of cloud by day, by night a pillar of fire,
Sons of the will, we fought the fight of the will our sire."

I shall try to give an account, necessarily brief and imperfect, of the successive steps by which this change in thought and feeling was brought about.

In the latter part of the eighteenth century there lived in London an artist named William Blake; a genius, self-taught, erratic, and ultimately quite crazy. He is chiefly known by his etchings, which were strange enough; but his writings are stranger still. One of the most remarkable of these writings is entitled *The Marriage of Heaven and Hell.* In this extraordinary little book, Blake takes up the old theory of the Manichæans or Gnostics, so well known to those who have studied the early history of the Christian church, and states it in terms of his own. There are in the universe, he says, two antagonistic principles: the force of vitality, commonly called evil, and the force of repression, commonly called good. Right living depends on a proper balancing of these two forces. Each has its place, and its equal place, in the world's order and the world's progress. That the principle of repression has been called good and that God has been identified with that side of life, while the principle of vitality is called evil and the spirit that underlies it is called the Devil, is a mere accident, due to the fact that all writers on morals have been either priests or lawyers, both of which classes are professional advocates of repression.

Blake's philosophy did not find many followers in England, either at the time or for a century afterward; though each of our two great American geniuses, Hawthorne and Poe, had a conception of the spiritual universe like that which has just been outlined. His first real successor is, I believe, Bernard Shaw, who shows the influence of this philosophy in several of his plays, and in one—*The Devil's Disciple*—frankly accepts Blake's view of life in its entirety. Blake is chiefly important to us as the one great English exponent of a movement which was at the time shaking the thought of Continental Europe to its foundations. In France, Rousseau was preaching in different words the same message as Blake, and finding converts by the thousand. The right of the individual to work out his own development in defiance of social traditions; the right of the living present to shake off the hand of the dead past; the essential importance of doing things, and the essential wrongness of trying to stop people from doing things because of mere conventions: these were the thoughts that Rousseau and Rousseau's followers were developing until they burst the bounds of all convention in the great Revolution of 1789. The same sort of thing was happening in Germany. This was the age which the historians of German literature designate as the *Sturm- und Drang-Periode*—the period of storm and stress. It was then that Schiller wrote his tragedy of *The Robbers*. It was then that Goethe conceived the original draft of his first part of *Faust*. In *The Robbers* Schiller voices the protest of the younger men of the day against the tyranny of external convention. In *Faust* Goethe pictures the spirit of a man striving to break down the shackles imposed upon him by his own finite nature and surroundings and asserting equality with the spirit of the universe. "Shall I quail before you, creature of flame?" says Faust to the embodied spirit of the world about him. "It is I, Faust, your equal"—no less bold in the assertion of equality because of the enormous disparity in power.

The day of storm and stress passed. The champions of individual freedom saw their theories tried in the French Revolution; and the results of that trial made the older and cooler heads among them ready to go back at least part way to the old rule of social conventions. Not that the voices which asserted the right to individual freedom and individual development were ever wholly stilled. The whole system of German transcendental philosophy was based upon the idea of the importance of the *ego*. And there were in every generation, from Fichte at the beginning of the nineteenth century to Nietzsche at the end of it, philosophers who preached the right of individual development in no uncertain terms. But for a long time they had slight influence on general literature and on the general thought of the men who were doing the world's work. Schiller's later dramas show a return to conventional types. The *Faust* of Goethe, as he took it up and developed it in his maturer years, is a wholly different conception from the *Faust* of the fragment. The new Faust still desires to widen his experience and to take within himself whatever of life the world has to provide; but his note toward the world and its spirit is no longer the bold note of challenge or defiance. It is the somewhat weary note of a man who feels that he has much to learn and relatively little satisfaction in learning it.

The poetry of the early part of the

nineteenth century, whatever its merits, makes no pretense of summoning the reader to vigorous action as a man. It is predominantly of the romantic school— the school which seeks its golden age in the past and which tries to take refuge from the evils of today in the contemplation of other and better things. The results of the French Revolution had discouraged people from preaching the doctrines on which that Revolution had been based. A poet like Wordsworth, who loves liberty, withdraws from the world of action into that of contemplation. A poet like Scott, who cares for the world of action and is not willing to withdraw from it, describes the ideals and aspirations of ages which had less liberty than we have today. Neither Wordsworth nor Scott has a definite message to the fighting men of the present. Wordsworth's message is to the men of the present who are not fighting, Scott's to the fighting men who are not of the present.

As always happens in such cases, the form of the poetry began to count for more and more, the substance for less and less. Poems, and to a less extent prose works, became masterpieces of literary art rather than bearers of a message. Southey, Byron, Moore, Shelley, Keats—where can you find a similar group of authors who wrote so much that was so good and yet left to the generation after them so little except a row of pictures on a wall? Nowhere unless it be the group of English novelists of a few years later—Bulwer, Dickens, Trollope, Thackeray. Small wonder that the Englishmen of the forties and the fifties who wished to make their reading a basis of action instead of a mere diversion grasped at the outspoken traditionalism of a Newman or of a Ruskin, who had something of vital concern in his heart! The message of a man like Newman or Ruskin might be right or it might be wrong; but it was in any event the word of some one who believed that God had given him something to preach to his fellow men. Therefore did men listen, and therefore did they feel bitter disappointment when they found that what Newman said and what Ruskin said did not in fact meet the needs of the age to which they preached. On the Continent of Europe, the "Young Hegelians" were addressing themselves vigorously to present-day problems; and for the time being their writings took powerful hold of the thought of Germany. But only faint echoes of this movement reached England.

Yet there was one great English poet of that day who had a message which did meet the needs of the age. This was Robert Browning. More fortunate than Newman or Ruskin, his face was turned toward the future instead of the past. He did not tell people that because the night was dark they must try to console themselves by the recollections of yesterday. He helped them to prepare for tomorrow as best they could. It was because he bore such a message and proffered real help to men who were trying to solve perplexing questions that he had power to make strong men listen to him, instead of to Swinburne or Morris or even Tennyson, who had the lyric form but had not the intellectual or emotional substance which people were craving.

Browning speaks to men who are trying to work out the problems of liberty. His poetry always, even at its worst, contains thoughts that help toward this end; and his better poems are written in such a way that they stimulate the emotions as well as the thoughts which are needed in the citizens of a free commonwealth. I say his better poems; for Browning, though fairly consistent as a thinker, is as a writer of English literature more unequal in his different works than anybody since John Bunyan.

Browning's philosophy of life was fairly outlined, though not fully developed, in 1835. In his *Paracelsus,* published in that year, he pictures the thoughts of a man bent on realizing what there was in himself and on giving others the opportunity to realize what there was in them; first admired, then hated, but always living, always going forward, and never so wholly triumphant as when he dies outcast by his fellows. Browning has gone back to Blake's conception of vitality as a thing essentially right and essentially necessary; but he avoids Blake's error of linking the name of God with the spirit of repression, and making him the God of only half the world, instead of the whole. God is not the God of conventions, though conventions may be necessary; he is not the God of the dead but of the living. "I have lived," says Paracelsus, when scoffing at the idea that God requires "Pardon of him because of praise denied"; "We only have to live to set forth God's praise." But the living must be something positive; not a mere impatience of restraint; not the petty law-breaking which constituted Shelley's idea of what living meant, nor the middle-sized law-breaking which pleases Bernard Shaw, nor even the gigantic law-breaking which Byron and afterward Swinburne liked to imagine; but the living out a life in which the aim for power goes hand in hand with the love of one's fellow men, and in which the disregard of laws and conventions is only the bursting of the husk when the seed develops into the plant.

To Blake the struggle between individual vitality and the conventions that repress it was necessarily a struggle between two antagonistic principles—just as it is to Bernard Shaw at the present day. Browning took a saner and, as it seems to me, a truer view of the nature of the conflict. There are certain things which the individual does to work out his own destiny. There are other things which organized society does to work out its own safety and permanence as an organization. An entire repression of the individual means stagnation; an entire disregard of social conventions in behalf of the individual means anarchy. Somewhere between the two we are bound to find a way of right living; not as a result of a balance between opposing forces, but as a point where the needs both of the individual and of society may be realized concurrently. The repression of the individual is not the end of the law. It is an incident—an undesirable incident but often a necessary one. Browning saw both sides of this issue as few poets, or, for the matter of that, few living men, have ever been able to see both sides of any issue. In *Bishop Blougram's Apology,* intellectually one of the most remarkable poems of the century, he gives us an illuminating discussion, between a Catholic priest and a literary free lance, concerning liberty of thought and the propriety of suppressing one's own individual convictions for the sake of an ulterior end to be obtained. Every man who reads this poem attentively will understand many fundamental things in life better than he did before. An even more varied insight is shown in *The Ring and The Book,* where the history of certain dark transactions is set forth as it looks from different standpoints—the injurer and the injured, the lawyer and the man who breaks the law from a desire to do right, with the pope's own summation of the complexity of the whole and the mixed rightness and wrongness of the different parts. For the struggle of life with which we have to deal is nothing so simple as a struggle between marshalled forces of vitality on one side and of repression on the other. It is a struggle where the vitality of one man craves for the restriction and repression of others; where we must balance the claims and demands of different kinds of men and women and the value of different kinds of social order. The poetry which the man of action in the twentieth century demands is poetry which will help him to understand his place in that struggle and inspire him to accept its burdens. It is because Browning does this that men read Browning when they are ceasing to read men among his contemporaries who were greater literary artists and greater masters of poetic style.

But how shall good and evil be determined when there is no pope to weigh the
motives? If Newman and Ruskin are
wrong in telling us to be guided by the
past, where shall a guide be found? These
were questions which poets and novelists
of the middle of the last century were
vainly trying to solve. The voice of complacency which had characterized the literature of the generation earlier had given
place to the voice of protest. Carlyle,
Kingsley, the Brontés, George Eliot, all
in their several ways, were expressing
cravings which the past had not satisfied
and asking questions to which tradition
furnished no answer. Browning showed
us how to find the answer in many particular cases; to the question in its broad form
even Browning did not give, or attempt to
give, a general answer.

The present generation thinks it has
found the way in which this answer is to

be reached. The contest between man and man or between system and system is not a purposeless agency of destruction. It is the means of proving which is the better man or which the better system. Where previous generations said, "Right must prevail in the long run," and held it as a somewhat dim article of religious faith, the present generation sets out to discover what is going to prevail in the long run, in the full confidence that if this can be found it will be right. And meantime, while it strives to regulate struggles and wars, it nevertheless accepts them, and to some degree glorifies them, as a means of proving all things that we may hold fast that which is good.

" Good luck to those who see the end !
    Good-bye to those that drown !
  To each his chance, as chance shall send,
    And God for all ! Shut down !"

That verse summarizes the theology of a large part of the church militant as it exists today.

But, you will ask, what is meant by characterizing this as a spiritual philosophy, or as a true philosophy of any kind? Is it not rather a glorification of brute force? If it be true that men feel thus and think thus, is it not a deplorable fact, full of danger for the future, rather than a source of spiritual hope and promise? Do not these doctrines normally result in an animalism like that of D'Annunzio or a cynicism like that of Bernard Shaw, rather than in zeal for moral truth and in high ideals of what the human race can be and ought to be?

This is a fair question, which needs to be squarely answered.

If we encourage people to follow out their own impulses, in the belief that time will show which impulses are good and which impulses are bad, men of strong animal instincts, with little judgment, will be tempted to pursue careers of lust or cruelty; and writers like D'Annunzio, who have strong passions and little self-control, will preach the doctrine that this exercise of liberty is the normal conduct of humanity—a sign of strength rather than of weakness. But this kind of career brings its own ruin; and this kind of literature carries with it its own refutation. The men who follow their passions find that they have taken the road to self-destruction, not the road to power. The men who have preached the gospel of animalism find that it is a gospel of decadence, not of life. If such a writer has eyes to see and a heart to feel, he gradually discovers the error of what he has done. The Zola of *L'Assommoir* and *Nana* gives place to the Zola of *La Débâcle*. The writer who began by dwelling on corruption with an apparent love of the corrupt, has ended by grasping, as few other men have grasped it, the lesson that moral corruption leads to the downfall of a people.

Again, the man of mere intellectual power, without strong human sympathies, may take this doctrine as an encouragement to treat life as a game, in which it is his sole duty to use his intelligence to win. And a writer of this temperament may take pleasure in analyzing life in this spirit, to the detriment of all serious purpose and serious feeling. This danger is more real than the other, because the unsympathetic man frequently gets a considerable measure of success and power, and the unsympathetic writer may continue writing for a long time before anything happens to disprove his views. Yet even with men of this type, the attempt to follow out consequences honestly and write stories truthfully gradually leads to higher instead of lower views of life. The early dramas of Bernard Shaw contained much amusing cynicism and little suggestion of anything better. In *Man and Superman* the cynicism has become, almost in spite of itself, a vehicle for conveying spiritual truth, none the less profound because of its unconventional or irreverent form. I know of nothing more striking in the way of philosophic preaching than in Satan's suggestion to the pious lady who has unexpectedly found herself in hell, that she should go to heaven and try living there for a while in order that she may see how uncomfortable she would be in such a place. When she asks with surprise whether she would be allowed to go and try, she is told that the only reason why anybody ever stays in hell is because hell is the only place for which they feel themselves suited. And when she inquires whether a great many souls do not stay in heaven a long time before they have found out their mistake, there is a terrible touch of truth as well as irony in Satan's answer, so characteristic of Bernard Shaw, that they are chiefly English souls who have been brought up to think that they were moral when they were only uncomfortable. The same evolution is seen in the case of one greater than Bernard Shaw, Ibsen. If ever there was a man whose genius was predominantly intellectual and whose passion was a passion for analysis, it was Henrik Ibsen. There was a time when people thought that his dramas undermined faith in humanity. We now see that what they chiefly undermined was our faith in shams; and that pitiless exposition of the consequences of what is weak in modern life may serve as a sure means to help us in deciding upon what we can hold to as really strong.

For after all the lesson which observation teaches to the man of brains is the same that instinct has taught the gentleman for many ages past: that in any conflict which is worthy of the name strength counts for less than intelligence, intelligence for less than discipline, discipline for less than self-sacrifice; or, to put it in positive words, that unswerving devotion is the thing that counts for most of all. The grim wager of battle is, as Carlyle says, full of glorious possibilities of life. Conflict is above and beyond all else a test of loyalty. The more complex the struggle, the more does the power to stand this test come into the foreground as the decisive element. This fact it is, more than all others, which makes the modern philosophy of conflict deserve the title of a spiritual philosophy. It is because our D'Annunzios and our Shaws fail to recognize this that they fall short of intellectual

104

greatness. It is because our Brownings and our Kiplings recognize this fact that they achieve a permanent hold on mankind.

If there is one message more than another with which modern English poetry is charged, it is this message of enduring loyally.

> " To see a good in evil, and a hope
>   In ill success"

is Browning's text.

> " Say not, 'The struggle naught availeth,
>   The labor and the wounds are vain;
> The enemy faints not, nor faileth,
>   And as things have been they remain.'
>
> " If hopes were dupes, fears may be liars;
>   It may be through yon smoke concealed
> Your comrades chase even now the flyers,
>   And but for you possess the field,"

sings Clough, a forerunner of the modern school of poetry, taken away from us, unfortunately, before the time of his full fruition. It is the inspiration of this message that lights up the bare rafters of the mess room of the cholera-stricken officers in Ceylon:

" So stand to your glasses steady,
    For this is a world of lies;
Here's a glass to the dead already
    And here's to the next that dies!"

It is this spirit that breathes through every line of Henley, and with which the poetry of Rudyard Kipling is so charged and surcharged that if I once began quoting from him I know not where I should stop.

"He that shall endure to the end, the same shall be saved." This is one of the great spiritual lessons of the militant school of poetry. And side by side with this there is another lesson, or group of lessons, equally important: the lesson of tolerance and of reverence.

If a man works out his philosophy of life by himself or with his books as his only companions, it is hard for him to avoid a good deal of injustice toward people whose convictions are different from his own. He may not always judge the past as the man did who started with the doctrine that whatever is is right, and drew the conclusion that whatever was was wrong. Nor will he always go to the same lengths as the Presbyterian divine who published a book in which he summarized the result of his reasonings under the title "The Final Philosophy." But the mode in which he has arrived at his convictions will make it, to say the least, very difficult for him to understand how any man of sense and honesty could ever have arrived at different ones. The man who has really had the chance to compare his views with other men's views will look at things in a broader way. Though his own feelings may be intense, he will know that other men are equally honest when they hold other views and feel other emotions. The very fact that he is willing to put his ideas to the test of conflict means that he is ready to give fair play to other men's ideas. If the things which were of use to a past generation are different from those that he thinks the present needs, he does not on that account despise them or brand them as fictions. If he is a man of any largeness of vision, he sees that the philosophy of the future will grow beyond what the present can conceive, just as the best conceptions of the present have grown beyond the possibilities of the past. He is content to let each man get at the right in his own way and use the forms of thought which help him most. What matter is it if MacAndrew's God be the result of a mixture of Calvinistic theology with the principles of steam engineering, while the Lama's God is the result of lonely meditation among the snow mountains concerning impossible stories of

Buddha? If God under these forms, or any other forms, can make engineers like MacAndrew and priests like the Lama and help them to know, as each knew in his way, the real sizes and values of the different parts of life, let us accept the result and be thankful that men have reached it by the roads that best suited their several feet.

> " How can I turn from any fire
>   On any man's hearthstone?
> I know the longing and desire
>   That went to build my own!"

A tolerance like this has nothing in common with the indifference of the man who plays with his convictions. It represents rather the seriousness of the man who values the essential part of his faith all the more because he feels how much greater is the reality for which he is striving than the imperfect representation of it which he already has achieved. For the poet of today, like the Hebrew poets of old, is essentially a prophet—the bearer of a progressive revelation; one of a historic chain of seers, feeling after God if haply they may find him, and each in his own way bringing men a little nearer to the truth.

" When I was a king and a mason, a master
      proven and skilled,
  I planned to build me a palace such as a king
      should build.
  I decreed and dug down to my levels; and,
      buried under the silt,
  I came on the wreck of a palace such as a king
      had built.

" There was no wit in the fashion, there was no
      worth in the plan;
  Hither and thither, aimless, the ruined footings
      ran;
  Masonry brute, mishandled, yet graven on
      every stone
  'After me cometh a builder; tell him, I too
      have known.'

" Swift to my use in the trenches where my well-
        planned groundworks grew
    I tumbled his quoins and his ashlars, I cut and
        reset them anew.
    Lime I had from his marbles, burned it, slaked
        it, and spread,
    Taking or leaving at pleasure the gifts of the
        humble dead.

" Yet I despised not or gloried; yet as we
        wrenched them apart
    I read in the razed foundations the heart of
        that builder's heart.
    As he had risen and pleaded, so did I under-
        stand
    The form of the dream he had followed by the
        face of the thing he had planned.

" When I was a king and a mason, in the open
        noon of my pride
    They sent me a word from the darkness; they
        whispered and called me aside.
    They said, 'The end is forbidden'; they said,
        'Thy use is fulfilled;
    Thy work shall be as the other's, the spoil of a
        king that shall build.'

" I called my men from my trenches, my quar-
ries, my wharves, and my sheers;
All I had wrought I abandoned to the faith of
the faithless years;
Only I carved on the timber, only I wrought
in the stone
*After me cometh a builder.   Tell him, I too
have known!*"

APPENDIX I

ON THE MEANING OF THE TERM PHILOSOPHY

WHEN these lectures were delivered I was asked by two or three persons what the word philosophy really meant. This is a much easier question to ask than to answer. A study of the definitions and the illustrative passages given in the Oxford Dictionary leads one to the conclusion that the English word philosophy can be used in as many different senses as Mark Twain found for the elusive German word *Zug;* which, as he truthfully remarked, could mean anything from a bank check to a railroad train. Under such circumstances each man may, within certain broad limits, choose his own definition. A philosophy, as I understand it, is a set of working hypotheses which a man adopts in order to harmonize, as far as may be, his prejudices with his experience.

There are certain ideas or prejudices which we accept without proof and take as starting points in our own reasoning. It is in this manner that we assume our own existence, the existence of other people like ourselves, the reality of an external world of some kind, and an underlying orderliness in the events of that world. None of these things is capable of proof, in the ordinary sense of the term. The *Cogito ergo sum* of Descartes does not represent the real reason for believing in a man's own existence. It is simply a means of making a belief which we already possess appear logically plausible. I know of no better name by which to call these assumptions than the old and somewhat abused term innate ideas. They are based on inherited habits of action and thought, which have lasted throughout so many generations that they have become unconscious if not instinctive. They represent prejudices rather than reasoned judgments regarding the universe; and they exemplify in a striking degree that superiority of prejudice over reason which Burke so cogently set forth.

Side by side with these innate ideas or prejudices there gradually come into our lives other ideas which we acquire consciously as the result of teaching and observation. Our own experience of everyday life and the truths of history and science which we learn from others supplement our preconceived notions of the universe, and as we grow older begin to conflict with them. Out of this conflict comes a readjustment of our prejudices. No man, however strong his innate ideas, holds them in quite the same form at thirty that he did at fifteen. But though men modify their preconceptions they never reject them. However much a man may become imbued with the facts of physics, he puts them in a framework of metaphysics of his own.

What holds true of an individual holds true of a community. A tribe starts with certain underlying ideas regarding the universe, usually expressed in the form of a religious creed. As the tribe grows into a nation its beliefs are modified by the events with which it comes in contact and its creeds are readjusted in the light of experience. The generation of Aeschylus had learned some things which prevented the creed of Homer from satisfying it. The generation of Aristotle had learned some things which prevented the creed of Aeschylus from satisfying it. There is a constant change in the kind of philosophy that meets a people's demands. The popular belief and prejudice of early times is like the system of the universe which presents itself to the mind of a child—based much on dreams and little on facts. The fully developed philosophy of a later day has discarded part, but never the whole, of the dream.

The attempt to get a system of working hypotheses which shall satisfy our instincts without conflicting with our experience is the most difficult problem which logic presents. For we are not trying to compare the validity of two similar kinds of proof, or even the results of two different kinds of evidence. We are adjusting a set of formulas derived from the inherited experience of the race to the limitations set by the acquired experience of the individual. The process of achieving this result is philosophy. The result, when we get it, is *a* philosophy—good or bad, as the case may be.

It has become a habit in modern times, particularly in the United States, to use the word philosophy in a somewhat narrower sense; to treat it as a branch of psychology, or as being at any rate subject-matter for the professed psychologist rather than for the man of letters or man of affairs. It is quite admissible to use the term in this sense if we so desire. Every event is essentially an impression made upon us by something external to ourselves. The study of the external world is the work of physical science. The study of the impressions we are receiving from that world constitutes an important part of the work of psychology. There is a tendency to confine the name philosophy to the conclusions derived from this study of mental impressions; and that tendency has acquired much force at the present day because two or three eminent psychologists, notably Herbert Spencer and Wil-

liam James, have developed brilliant philosophies of life which are based upon the
study of psychology and which ignore, if
they do not defy, the dictates of logical
convention. But the majority of men who
have helped to formulate the thought of
the world regarding the relation between
its instincts and its experience have been
logicians rather than psychologists. The
great names in the history of philosophy during past ages—Plato, Aristotle,
Aquinas, Descartes, Spinoza, Kant—have
all been primarily logicians. Their work
as psychologists has been incidental. With
one or two, like Plato or perhaps Spinoza,
psychology has been a highly important
and useful incident of their studies; with
the others it has been a secondary, or even
(as in the case of Descartes) a somewhat
detrimental incident.

We shall, I believe, get a truer conception of the work of the philosophic think-

ers of the past if we regard the problem as a logical instead of a psychological one—based on a study of evidence rather than on a study of mental processes.

APPENDIX II

THE INFLUENCE OF CHARLES DAR-
WIN ON HISTORICAL AND
POLITICAL SCIENCE

THE theories of Charles Darwin
found readier and prompter acceptance among historians than among biologists.

When Darwin presented the doctrine
of natural selection to the zoölogists and
botanists he was confronting them with a
new set of scientific ideas and conceptions.
His contemporaries were reluctant to
accept these new ideas. They had been
brought up to regard different species as
having been created independently. The
idea that types could be modified by slow
process of change was something foreign
to their minds. The idea that existing

types simply represented the result of successful experiment in a field where the unsuccessful experiments had been eliminated by death was still more novel and repugnant. It was not until the generation after Darwin that his fellow biologists as a class were ready to abandon the idea of special acts of creation for specific purposes and to search instead for the slow operation of natural causes.

In history and in politics the case was different. All students of history accepted the idea of evolution in their own field of special study; most of them regarded historical evolution as the result of a process of natural selection.

Without an underlying idea of evolution human history is a meaningless chronicle, unworthy of the attention of intelligent men. If different historical events were independent of one another there would be no sense in writing history at all.

122

All serious investigators in this field, from Thucydides and Aristotle down to the present time, have sought either to develop the details of this orderly and gradual evolution or to lay down the principles of its operation. The man who today reads the *Politics of Aristotle* for the first time will be struck by the prevalence of methods of thought which many biologists suppose Darwin to have invented. And the same idea of evolution thus used by Aristotle has been applied in varying forms by all who sought to develop a philosophy of history—by Hegel and his followers in Germany or by men of the type of Henry Thomas Buckle in England.

Not only was the idea of evolution thus familiar to the historians; the idea of natural selection was also prominent in the minds of many of them. The whole doctrine of John Stuart Mill concerning liberty was founded upon reliance on a process of natural selection. Look for your hero in all possible directions, he said, and you get the best chance of finding him. The issue between Mill and Carlyle reminds one of the controversies between Darwinian and anti-Darwinian in the field of biology. Carlyle believed in the special creation of a number of individual heroes; Mill, together with nearly all scientifically trained historians, believed in the evolution of heroes by natural selection.

The conception of economic or political conflict as a means of determining the survival of the fittest was seen perhaps even more conspicuously in Malthus's theory of population—a theory which Darwin himself regarded as having in some respects foreshadowed his own work. Malthus based his whole treatment of political economy upon the doctrine that population tended to outrun subsistence; that the struggle for existence was a constant pro-

124

cess of elimination of the weak; and that any attempt to interfere with this process resulted rather in the deterioration than in the improvement of the peoples that it was designed to benefit.

If then the idea of evolution had been a fundamental one in historical and political science for more than two thousand years, and if the idea of elimination by natural selection was by no means unfamiliar to political thinkers, what was there left for the followers of Darwin to do in this field?

They found at least two things to do. In the first place, they showed how natural selection was a means of developing, not only *individuals* of superior ability or intelligence, but *types* of superior adaptation to their surroundings; and they taught us further to regard this adaptation of the type to its surroundings as the thing which gave it its right to exist.

The first of these points is well illustrated by the history of the Malthusian theory before and after Darwin. Malthus and almost all the Malthusians before the time of Darwin talked of an actual struggle for food between different individuals. They thought that there was not enough food to go round, and that this fact was a direct means of keeping workers up to a certain standard of efficiency and prudence by the direct elimination of the weak. Today we see that the result is far more indirect than this. There is, in civilized communities at least, no habitual scarcity of food. This has been avoided by the development of certain institutions like the family and private property and certain motives which go with those institutions which prevent the scarcity that would otherwise exist. A generation ago the critics of Malthus thought that the non-existence of the scarcity disproved the

126

Malthusian theory. Today we see that it confirms it. It shows that the type has adapted itself to its environment.

It is the institution even more than the man that has been marked out for survival by the process of natural selection. We have known for generations how elimination affected the development of individuals. It was Darwin who taught us to account in this way for the growth of species—in history as well as in biology. And in thus accounting for the origin and growth of institutions, he furnished for the first time an objective justification of the ethical standards and motives by which those institutions were upheld. Every prominent political thinker before Darwin, with the one notable exception of Edmund Burke, referred historical events to some preconceived ethical standard of his own, and judged them to be good or bad according as they conformed to his preconceived ideas. This is true even of a man like John Stuart Mill. He had great natural love of liberty, and was essentially tolerant in his disposition. Yet one can feel in all his work the underlying assumption that the chief reason for approving of liberty is its effect in developing the type of character represented by the liberal and tolerant Englishman of the nineteenth century.

This attitude of mind was a great help to Mill in arranging a coherent system of political economy; and as long as he addressed an audience whose general views and general standards were like his own, it enabled him to appeal to them with great force. But the instant he was brought face to face with a protectionist like Carey or a socialist like Lassalle, what had previously been an element of strength became an element of weakness. There was no common ground from which to reason, and no means of finding any. It was

Darwin who furnished the common
ground. It was Darwin who gave the
historians and political thinkers the pos-
sibility of reaching objective results from
their discussion which were previously
unattainable. You like one kind of man
and one kind of institution; I like another
kind of man or another kind of institution.
Very well; let us set to work to discover
which, in the long run, is going to prevail
over the other. That which will prevail
in the long run must be right. This is for
the historian the center and gist of Darwinism. We all assumed that orderly
evolution existed; we most of us understood a good deal about a process of natural selection which was going on. But
none of us until Darwin came had learned
to take the results of natural selection as a
standard; to make the fact of permanence
the test of the right to remain; to assume
the view of the philosophical pragmatist

in dealing with the problems that came before us.

Of course this is a doctrine that needs to be applied with great care. The frank acceptance of survival as a test of right is attended with the danger that we may take too short periods of history under our observation, and may think that an idea or an institution has won the race when it is riding most hurriedly toward its downfall. But in spite of all these dangers, the necessity of applying the survival test compels the man who is naturally dogmatic to be somewhat less so, and helps the man who is naturally objective to be somewhat more so. It is a restraint upon the man who does not want to have to prove his points; it is an assistance to the man who does.

This change in modes of thought and criteria of ethics did not come suddenly. It was far easier for popular writers to seize upon certain results of Darwin's thinking and try to apply them to history in the form of rhetorical analogies than it was to get at the Darwinian habit of mind in dealing with historical problems in general. Herbert Spencer's writings furnish a very marked instance of this error. Spencer's style was so felicitous and his works were so widely read that he did a good deal to retard the application of the really important results of Darwin's work to political thinking. Spencer and his followers made much of the conception of society as an organism; but they overlooked the fact that historians had been treating society as an organism for more than two thousand years. In the belief that they had occupied a new field, they permitted themselves to employ a number of loose analogies, in total ignorance of the fact that competent observers had already gone over much of the ground by scientific methods. Historians had been proving which forms of social life *did* survive; and this proof, defective or uncertain as it was in many instances, was yet better than the guesses of the Spencerian, on the basis of remote analogy, as to which forms of social life *were going to* survive. When Spencer pronounced evolution good or bad according as it did or did not "proceed from an incoherent indefinite homogeneity to a coherent definite heterogeneity," he was writing down in large letters the fact that he was born a good while before *The Origin of Species* had appeared. He had put on a few of the external attributes of the modern biologist; that was all. The hands were the hands of Esau, but the voice was the voice of Jacob. Or, to take an instance from a different field: when W. K. Clifford, in his now almost forgotten *Lectures and Essays,* proclaimed the right and duty of the unlimited exercise of private judgment, and called down anathemas on the head of every man who wished to exercise his own private judgment to the extent of differing from Mr. W. K. Clifford in this particular, he simply showed that he lived too early to have felt the full effect of *The Origin of Species* in leading people to substitute objective criteria for subjective ones.

But it would perhaps be more to the purpose to give instances of writers who were influenced by Darwin, instead of those who were not.

Among English economists, the man who was quickest to feel the force of the new movement was Walter Bagehot. Bagehot's Darwinian ideas are popularly known from his *Physics and Politics*—an interesting and often exceedingly brilliant set of conjectures regarding the operation of survival in prehistoric periods. But

Bagehot's main work and main interest were always in the nearer parts of history, and particularly economic history, rather than the remoter parts. He it was who, in an age when England still followed John Stuart Mill blindly, first questioned the general admissibility of Mill's assumptions. In these twentieth century days, when competition is regarded, not as an axiom or postulate of political economy, but simply as an important incident in its development, it is difficult for us to understand the courage that was involved forty years ago in publishing two critical essays in which competition was regarded, not as a standard to which all things must conform, but as one among several alternative phases or modes of social service, whose relative claims were to be investigated and relative merits judged by their applicability to given conditions. In this mental attitude the English writer who has followed

Bagehot most closely is W. J. Ashley, whose *English Economic History* may be taken as furnishing a clear exemplification of Darwin's influence upon the methods of modern economic thought.

Meantime a German investigator in economics, Adolph Wagner of Berlin, had been taking up Darwinian methods on a larger scale and applying them with conspicuous success. Wagner may be said to have developed his Darwinism at the opposite end from Bagehot. Bagehot had been brought up in the methods of the deductive school of economics, and was impressed with their inapplicability; Wagner had been accustomed to the methods of the historical school of economics, and was impressed with their inconclusiveness. While Bagehot wanted to make his analysis broad enough to fit different kinds of facts, Wagner was concerned to make his synthesis coherent enough to bring him to some positive proofs and conclusions. Wagner's treatment of the theory of property right is a good example of his philosophical method. He rejects both the crude juristic theory that property right is based upon occupancy and the equally crude philosophic theory that it ought to be based on labor. Society has established property right because it has shown itself the best motive—in fact, apparently the necessary motive—in order to get industry well and efficiently managed. It is only by the application of this last theory that you can make a connection between what is and what ought to be; between your history and economics on the one hand and your law and ethics on the other. If the philosopher says that property ought to be based upon labor, the jurist can laugh at him. If the jurist says that property is based upon occupancy or upon the constitution of society, the philosopher can say that the occupants are bad men and that the sooner society changes its constitution the better. But if property is an institution which has survived while other forms of social organization have failed, because property preserves nations and socialism destroys them, then socialism is disproved by the logic of events—the logic that Darwin has taught us to apply to problems of this kind.

It is, however, not so much in its special applications that the Darwinian theory has affected modern political science as in the general habit of mind which it has fostered and cultivated. It has not led to many great discoveries which can be set apart from the general run of facts previously known; but it has led to changes in the methods of judgment which enable us to understand and use all historical facts in a more objective way.

A few years ago, when Dr. Jowett was

master of Balliol, there was a discussion
concerning two men who had attained high
position at an early age. One of them had
become a bishop, the other a judge; and
the conversation turned on the respective
merits of the two careers. One of the dons
said: "I prefer the bishop. The judge can
only say, 'You be hanged'; the bishop can
say, 'You be damned.'" "Yes," said Dr.
Jowett, sententiously, "but when the judge
says, 'You be hanged,' *you are hanged.*"
The influence of Charles Darwin on historical and political thought may be
summed up by saying that he has made our
historians cease to aspire to be bishops
and content themselves with the more
modest but also more effective position of
judges. For broad principles of judgment
which they could not apply effectively they
have substituted narrower but clearer ones
whose application can be made evident to
their fellow men.

I have spoken of this attitude of mind as having been foreshadowed in the works of Edmund Burke. To him, as to the modern thinker, human history was the record of a process of elimination and survival. To him political institutions and political ideas had grown up as a means of preserving the race that held them. And to him also it was unwarrantable to attempt to tear down on *a priori* grounds beliefs and methods that had preserved the race that held them, unless you were able to substitute something practically better in their place. A thing did not seem to him correct which was logically good and practically bad. He suspected a defect in the logic. Was he right or wrong? In the first half of the nineteenth century the majority of men would have said that he was from a theoretical standpoint wrong. They admired his insight into the political conditions of his day, but they would have none of his theories. Today the world feels a little less sure about some of his individual judgments than it did at the time when they were uttered; but as a matter of theory it has accepted his method as a sound one. It is in general prepared to make survival a test of right.

This is Darwin's contribution to political science; and the completeness with which this contribution is accepted is shown by the sudden cessation of public interest in books which do not apply or accept that test. Students of politics no longer read either Hegel or Comte. Buckle's *History of Civilization*, which in the years immediately following its appearance had a greater success than Darwin's *Origin of Species*, is now known only to a few specialists in English literature. Mill's *Principles of Political Economy* is valued for its contributions to the theory of banking;

but as a work of political philosophy it has lost the place which its author, modest man though he was, confidently claimed for it.

We can get a curious idea of the kind of change which has taken place by comparing two works which are closely akin, by two men who were closely associated— Mill on *Liberty* and Morley on *Compromise*. The two writers deal with nearly the same topic. They approach it with nearly the same prepossessions. They arrive at almost exactly the same practical conclusions. Yet Morley is read today, and Mill, speaking broadly, is not. Why? Because Mill is constantly referring things to a subjective standard, and Morley to an objective one. Mill's whole argument is essentially an *argumentum ad hominem,* even when it takes the form of an appeal to experience; Morley's an appeal to experience, even when it takes the form of an *argumentum ad hominem*.

We may not be any more correct in our political reasoning than our fathers. I dare say that when the world contrasts the political philosophy of today with that of a generation or two ago it will reprove us for our crude judgments and for the irreverence with which we have cast aside work that was better than our own because it did not reach its results by our methods. But we are at least trying as no previous generation has tried to get *objective* standards on which different men and different ages can agree; and for this effort, and for whatever measure of success it has attained, we may thank Charles Darwin.

INDEX

INDEX